# WORSHIP SONGS FOR TWO

## 8 FAVORITES FOR ONE PIANO, FOUR HANDS

— PIANO LEVEL —
INTERMEDIATE

ISBN 978-1-5400-1338-5

**HAL•LEONARD**®
7777 W. BLUEMOUND RD. P.O. BOX 13819 MILWAUKEE, WI 53213

Visit Hal Leonard Online at
**www.halleonard.com**

Visit Phillip at
**www.phillipkeveren.com**

## PREFACE

Playing duets is one of the richest rewards of playing the piano. Designed to be a solo instrument, it also provides the perfect landscape for collaborative music making. I have fond memories of the duet partners with whom I've shared the bench over the decades, and the occasions for which the music was prepared and presented.

This collection features some of the best contemporary worship songs, and my hope is that these arrangements will be useful in private and congregational settings alike.

*Phillip Keveren*

## BIOGRAPHY

Phillip Keveren, a multi-talented keyboard artist and composer, has composed original works in a variety of genres from piano solo to symphonic orchestra. Mr. Keveren gives frequent concerts and workshops for teachers and their students in the United States, Canada, Europe, and Asia. Mr. Keveren holds a B.M. in composition from California State University Northridge and a M.M. in composition from the University of Southern California.

# AMAZING GRACE
## (My Chains Are Gone)

Words by JOHN NEWTON
Traditional American Melody
Additional Words and Music by
CHRIS TOMLIN and LOUIE GIGLIO
Arranged by Phillip Keveren

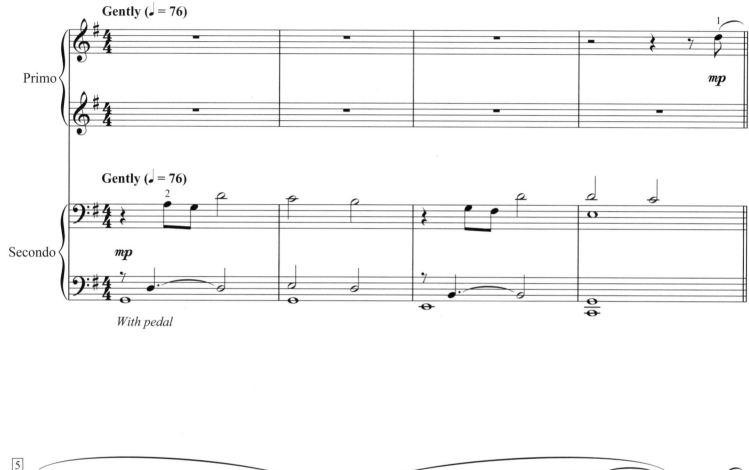

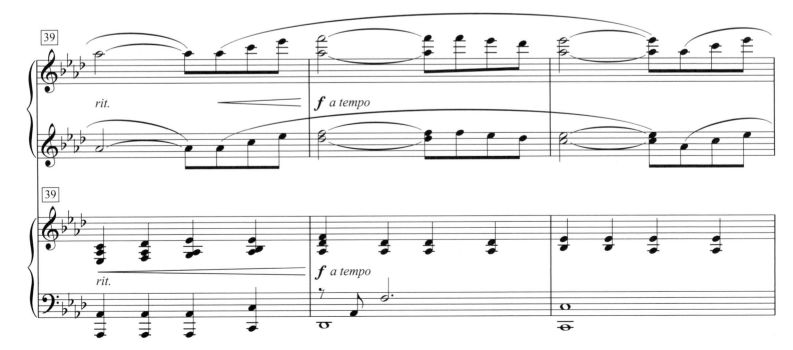

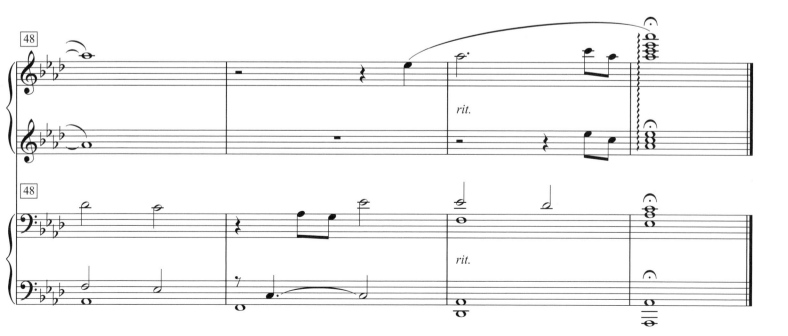

# CORNERSTONE

Words and Music by JONAS MYRIN,
REUBEN MORGAN, ERIC LILJERO
and EDWARD MOTE
Arranged by Phillip Keveren

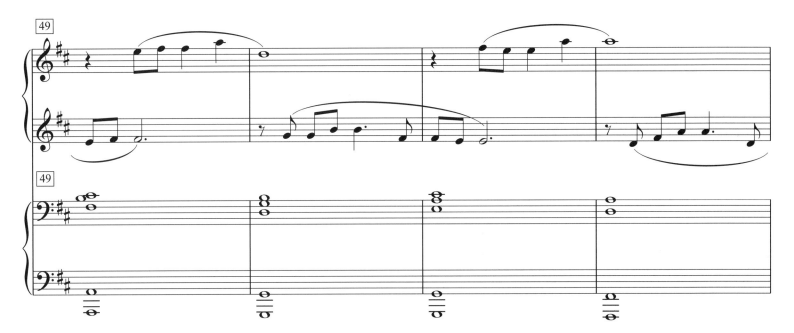

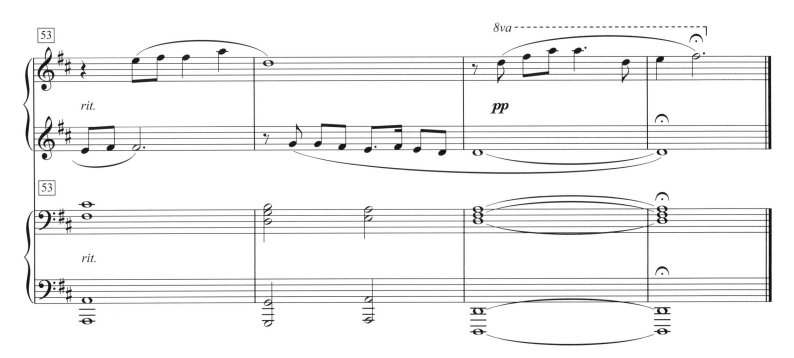

# FOREVER
## (We Sing Hallelujah)

Words and Music by BRIAN JOHNSON,
CHRISTA BLACK GIFFORD, GABRIEL WILSON,
JENN JOHNSON, JOEL TAYLOR and KARI JOBE
Arranged by Phillip Keveren

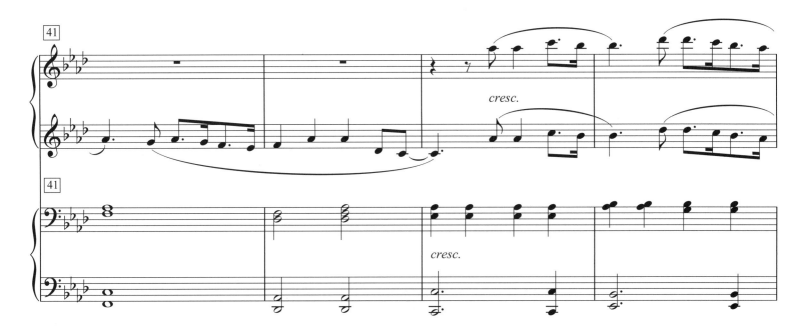

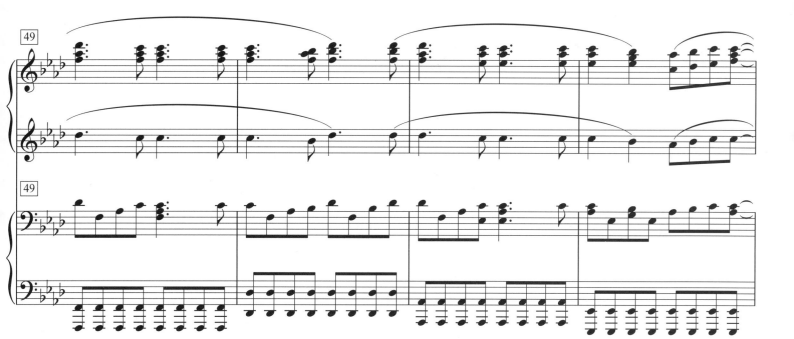

# GREAT I AM

Words and Music by
JARED ANDERSON
Arranged by Phillip Keveren

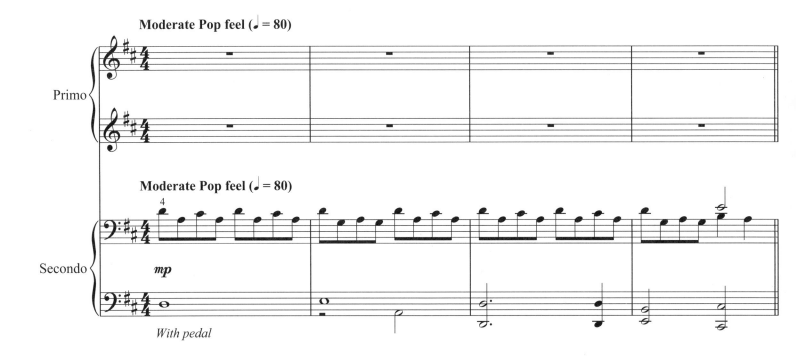

# IN CHRIST ALONE

Words and Music by KEITH GETTY
and STUART TOWNEND
Arranged by Phillip Keveren

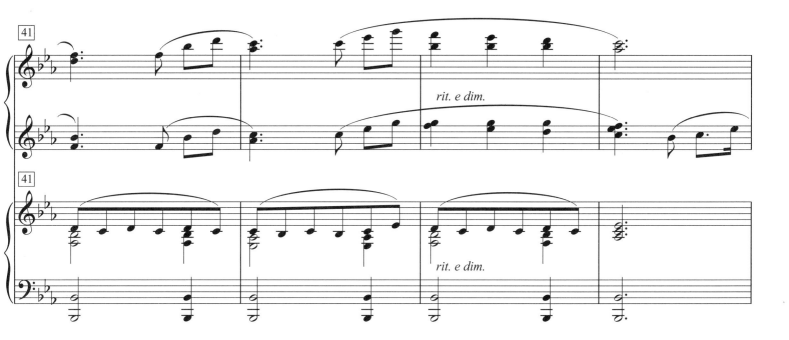

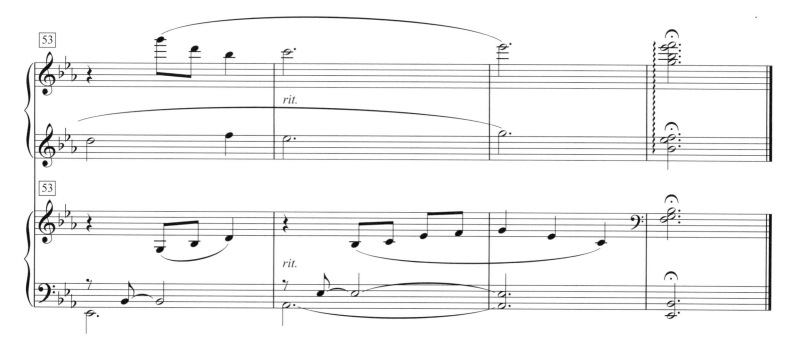

# THE LION AND THE LAMB

Words and Music by BRENTON BROWN,
BRIAN JOHNSON and LEELAND MOORING
Arranged by Phillip Keveren

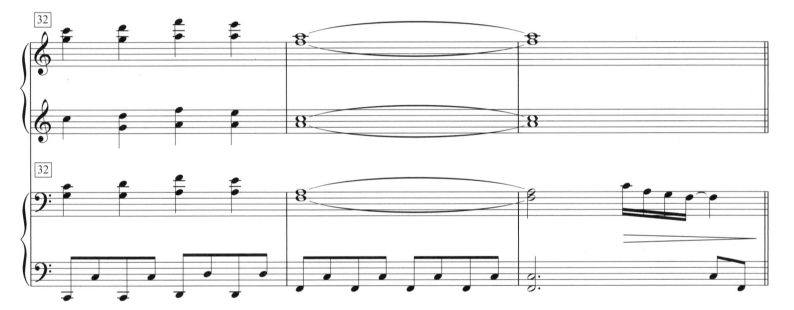

# LORD, I NEED YOU

Words and Music by JESSE REEVES,
KRISTIAN STANFILL, MATT MAHER,
CHRISTY NOCKELS and DANIEL CARSON
Arranged by Phillip Keveren

38

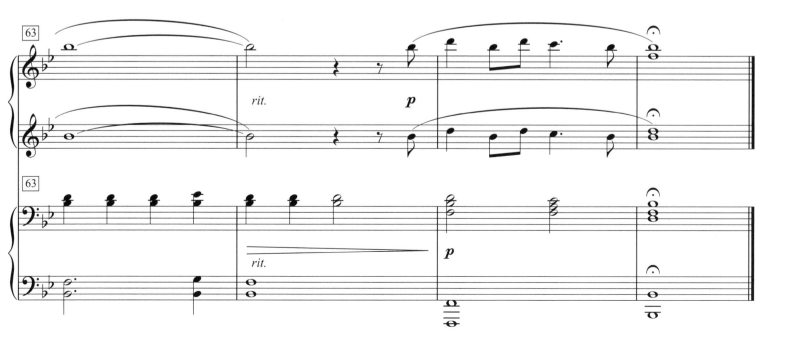

# 10,000 REASONS
## (Bless the Lord)

Words and Music by JONAS MYRIN
and MATT REDMAN
Arranged by Phillip Keveren

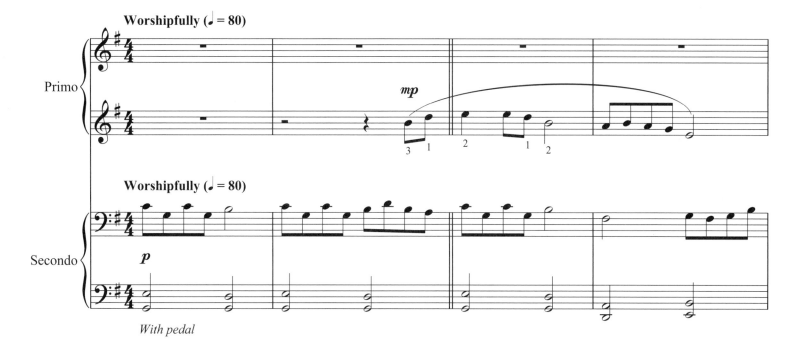

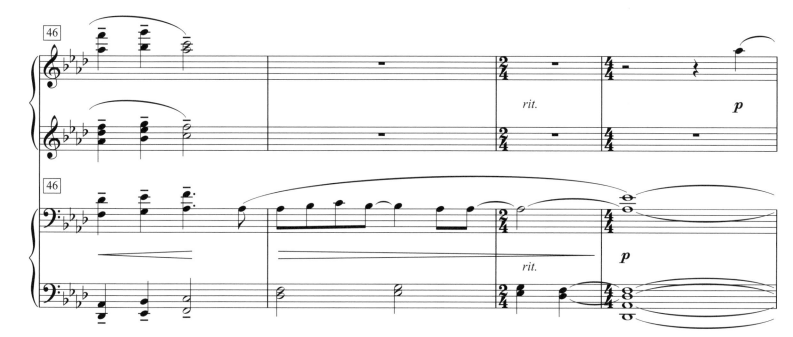

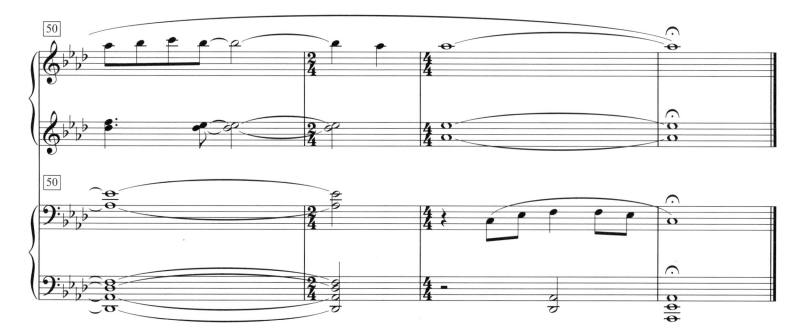

# THE PHILLIP KEVEREN SERIES

## PIANO SOLO

**ABBA FOR CLASSICAL PIANO**
00156644.....................................................$14.99

**ABOVE ALL**
00311024.....................................................$11.95

**AMERICANA**
00311348.....................................................$10.95

**BACH MEETS JAZZ**
00198473.....................................................$14.99

**THE BEATLES**
00306412.....................................................$16.99

**THE BEATLES FOR CLASSICAL PIANO**
00312189.....................................................$14.99

**BEST PIANO SOLOS**
00312546.....................................................$14.99

**BLESSINGS**
00156601.....................................................$12.99

**BLUES CLASSICS**
00198656.....................................................$12.99

**BROADWAY'S BEST**
00310669.....................................................$14.99

**A CELTIC CHRISTMAS**
00310629.....................................................$12.99

**THE CELTIC COLLECTION**
00310549.....................................................$12.95

**CHRISTMAS PRAISE HYMNS**
00236669.....................................................$12.99

**CHRISTMAS MEDLEYS**
00311414.....................................................$12.99

**CHRISTMAS AT THE MOVIES**
00312190.....................................................$14.99

**CHRISTMAS SONGS FOR CLASSICAL PIANO**
00233788.....................................................$12.99

**CHRISTMAS WORSHIP MEDLEYS**
00311769.....................................................$12.99

**CINEMA CLASSICS**
00310607.....................................................$14.99

**CLASSIC WEDDING SONGS**
00311101.....................................................$10.95

**CLASSICAL JAZZ**
00311083.....................................................$12.95

**COLDPLAY FOR CLASSICAL PIANO**
00137779.....................................................$14.99

**CONTEMPORARY WEDDING SONGS**
00311103.....................................................$12.99

**DISNEY SONGS FOR CLASSICAL PIANO**
00311754.....................................................$16.99

**FIDDLIN' AT THE PIANO**
00315974 ....................................................$12.99

**THE FILM SCORE COLLECTION**
00311811.....................................................$14.99

**GOSPEL GREATS**
00144351.....................................................$12.99

**THE GREAT AMERICAN SONGBOOK**
00183566.....................................................$12.99

**THE GREAT MELODIES**
00312084 ....................................................$12.99

**GREAT STANDARDS**
00311157.....................................................$12.95

**THE HYMN COLLECTION**
00311071.....................................................$12.99

**HYMN MEDLEYS**
00311349.....................................................$12.99

**HYMNS WITH A TOUCH OF JAZZ**
00311249.....................................................$12.99

**I COULD SING OF YOUR LOVE FOREVER**
00310905.....................................................$12.95

**JINGLE JAZZ**
00310762.....................................................$14.99

**BILLY JOEL FOR CLASSICAL PIANO**
00175310.....................................................$14.99

**ELTON JOHN FOR CLASSICAL PIANO**
00126449.....................................................$14.99

**LET FREEDOM RING!**
00310839.....................................................$9.95

**ANDREW LLOYD WEBBER**
00313227.....................................................$15.99

**MANCINI MAGIC**
00313523.....................................................$12.99

**MORE DISNEY SONGS FOR CLASSICAL PIANO**
00312113.....................................................$15.99

**THE MOST BEAUTIFUL SONGS FOR EASY CLASSICAL PIANO**
00233740.....................................................$12.99

**MOTOWN HITS**
00311295.....................................................$12.95

**PIAZZOLLA TANGOS**
00306870.....................................................$14.99

**POP STANDARDS FOR EASY CLASSICAL PIANO**
00233739.....................................................$12.99

**QUEEN FOR CLASSICAL PIANO**
00156645.....................................................$14.99

**RICHARD RODGERS CLASSICS**
00310755.....................................................$12.95

**SHOUT TO THE LORD!**
00310699.....................................................$12.95

**SONGS FROM CHILDHOOD FOR EASY CLASSICAL PIANO**
00233688.....................................................$12.99

**THE SOUND OF MUSIC**
00119403.....................................................$14.99

**SYMPHONIC HYMNS FOR PIANO**
00224738.....................................................$14.99

**TREASURED HYMNS FOR CLASSICAL PIANO**
00312112.....................................................$14.99

**THE TWELVE KEYS OF CHRISTMAS**
00144926.....................................................$12.99

**WORSHIP WITH A TOUCH OF JAZZ**
00294036.....................................................$12.99

**YULETIDE JAZZ**
00311911.....................................................$17.99

## EASY PIANO

**AFRICAN-AMERICAN SPIRITUALS**
00310610.....................................................$10.99

**CATCHY SONGS FOR PIANO**
00218387.....................................................$12.99

**CELTIC DREAMS**
00310973.....................................................$10.95

**CHRISTMAS CAROLS FOR EASY CLASSICAL PIANO**
00233686.....................................................$12.99

**CHRISTMAS POPS**
00311126.....................................................$14.99

**CLASSIC POP/ROCK HITS**
00311548.....................................................$12.95

**A CLASSICAL CHRISTMAS**
00310769.....................................................$10.95

**CLASSICAL MOVIE THEMES**
00310975.....................................................$10.99

**CONTEMPORARY WORSHIP FAVORITES**
00311805.....................................................$14.99

**DISNEY SONGS FOR EASY CLASSICAL PIANO**
00144352.....................................................$12.99

**EARLY ROCK 'N' ROLL**
00311093.....................................................$10.99

**EASY WORSHIP MEDLEYS**
00311997.....................................................$12.99

**FOLKSONGS FOR EASY CLASSICAL PIANO**
00160297.....................................................$12.99

**GEORGE GERSHWIN CLASSICS**
00110374.....................................................$12.99

**GOSPEL TREASURES**
00310805.....................................................$12.99

**THE VINCE GUARALDI COLLECTION**
00306821.....................................................$14.99

**HYMNS FOR EASY CLASSICAL PIANO**
00160294.....................................................$12.99

**IMMORTAL HYMNS**
00310798.....................................................$10.95

**JAZZ STANDARDS**
00311294.....................................................$12.99

**LOVE SONGS**
00310744.....................................................$10.95

**RAGTIME CLASSICS**
00311293.....................................................$10.95

**SONGS OF INSPIRATION**
00103258.....................................................$12.99

**SWEET LAND OF LIBERTY**
00310840.....................................................$10.99

**TIMELESS PRAISE**
00310712.....................................................$12.95

**10,000 REASONS**
00126450.....................................................$14.99

**TV THEMES**
00311086.....................................................$12.99

**21 GREAT CLASSICS**
00310717.....................................................$12.99

**WEEKLY WORSHIP**
00145342.....................................................$16.99

## BIG-NOTE PIANO

**CHILDREN'S FAVORITE MOVIE SONGS**
00310838.....................................................$12.99

**CHRISTMAS MUSIC**
00311247.....................................................$10.95

**CONTEMPORARY HITS**
00310907.....................................................$12.99

**HOW GREAT IS OUR GOD**
00311402.....................................................$12.95

**INTERNATIONAL FOLKSONGS**
00311830.....................................................$12.99

**JOY TO THE WORLD**
00310888.....................................................$10.95

**THE NUTCRACKER**
00310908.....................................................$10.99

## BEGINNING PIANO SOLOS

**AWESOME GOD**
00311202.....................................................$12.99

**CHRISTIAN CHILDREN'S FAVORITES**
00310837.....................................................$12.99

**CHRISTMAS FAVORITES**
00311246.....................................................$10.95

**CHRISTMAS TRADITIONS**
00311117.....................................................$10.99

**EASY HYMNS**
00311250.....................................................$12.99

**EVERLASTING GOD**
00102710.....................................................$10.99

**KIDS' FAVORITES**
00310822.....................................................$12.99

## PIANO DUET

**CLASSICAL THEME DUETS**
00311350.....................................................$10.99

**HYMN DUETS**
00311544.....................................................$12.99

**PRAISE & WORSHIP DUETS**
00311203.....................................................$11.95

**STAR WARS**
00119405.....................................................$14.99

Visit **www.halleonard.com**
for a complete series listing.

*Prices, contents, and availability
subject to change without notice.*

0917